How to Get that Job!

Andrie Penta

CONTENTS

To Philip, Evelyn and Nefeli. The ones who filled the chapters of my life with love, laughter, and unwavering support.

To Mum, Dad & Sister for the inspiration they have showered upon me.

INTRODUCTION

I'm excited to share my incredible journey of transformation from having nothing to being paid for pursuing my greatest passion. My life has been a whirlwind of experiences, each teaching me invaluable insights into the world of business and the mindset of large corporations. I'm thrilled to pass on these lessons through the pages of this book.

In the face of adversity, I discovered the art of turning lemons into lemonade. I embraced risks that ultimately shaped my identity today. Through collaboration with renowned international brands, I've not only grown as a professional but also as an individual.

Embarking on a job hunt is a challenging endeavor, especially after a prolonged break from work. Securing a job isn't just a task; it's a strategic venture that demands meticulous planning, thorough preparation, and skillful execution. At this stage in my career, I've transcended the need to search for jobs. Instead, I've charted a path where I'm compensated for indulging in my passions and selecting projects that truly resonate with me.

INTRODUCTION

Life itself is a gift, and finding a job that brings joy and fulfillment adds to the beauty of our existence on this planet. Bear in mind that the average person allocates approximately eight hours each day to their job, equating to roughly one-third of our entire lifetimes. Ensuring that these hours hold significance and provide a sense of fulfillment becomes exceptionally important.

Whether you're fresh out of college or a seasoned professional seeking a change, this guide is your compass to navigate the complex landscape of job hunting. Drawing from my personal journey, I'll guide you through each step, from crafting a remarkable resume to excelling in interviews and skillfully negotiating offers. Securing a job is a symphony of self-awareness preparation, and effective communication.

By adhering to the meticulously crafted steps in this guide, you'll be superbly equipped to maneuver through the job search labyrinth and secure a role that aligns with your skills, passions, and aspirations. Remember that each stage, regardless of the outcome, offers an opportunity for growth and learning.

Wishing you the best of luck on your remarkable job search mission!

Love

Andrie Penta

Chapter 1

SELF ASSESSMENT AND GOAL SETTING

I grew up in a family clothing business that included both retail stores and wholesale operations. At the age of 9, I was fully capable of running a (small) store by myself. I was taught how to welcome clients, guide them through the store, explain how clothing sizes worked, use the cash register, and perform a stock take.

My parents had me at a very young age and around that time they both decided to leave their well-paying jobs to become entrepreneurs. I was a first-row spectator of how a successful business is built. I was one of those kids that knew nothing different to long hours of work, 150% effort to make things happen and making every possible effort to making the family business a success.

Public holidays were the only days off, and thus, school breaks were workdays. I was a happy kid. I was aware that there was a reason and an objective for all that work. My father worked primarily on ideas and in sales. My mother was very analytical and loved numbers. I took after my dad. My inclination was to talk to people and establish connections, which inevitably resulted in sales and, ultimately, bigger sales. I was the one who successfully sold ice to an Eskimo. At the age of 14, I developed into one of the company's top sales performers. I loved sales. I had goals and the means to fulfill them.

It was incredibly gratifying for a young girl like me. My parents spotted those skills in me, very early on. We had thus commonly decided that I should study "Marketing and Management". It was a relatively new area of study at the time, and it seemed quite interesting. After all, that was what I was skilled at.

Little did I know of course. The age-old wisdom of "Man plans, and God laughs" became strikingly relevant. The enduring 20-year-old family enterprise, to which we dedicated considerable time and effort, suddenly experienced a substantial blow due to the decline in the local stock market.

The pricey education in Paris that was intended for me was no longer financially feasible for us. Naturally, the lessons in French which I was taking still held standing value, and the knowledge accumulated from my involvement in the family business since childhood would always remain perpetually relevant.

My strengths should be utilized. I had personal goals, and I would not give up because of a downturn. Afterall, I love challenges. Whenever things become stagnant, I get bored. With my parents' guidance and support, at the age of 17 I took a personal loan of £10K, which my godmother and godfather guaranteed, got on a plane on my own and headed to London.

I had secured a spot at the UK Universities' clearance session and was about to fulfill my dreams. Nothing would and could stand in my way. A week after my arrival in London, I understood that the funds I had obtained through the loan, along with some petty cash from my parents, would barely be enough to cover the first year's tuition and the on-campus room I would be renting. I needed warm clothing (coming from Cyprus-a very hot country), books, bedding, kitchen supplies, weekly travel passes, and food, of course. I started to feel anxious. My parents were facing eviction from our home, and they were getting a divorce. They needed to figure out how to support themselves individually while also caring for my younger sister who was still at school. I had nothing to anticipate. I had to work things out for myself.

At that time, I met a true friend. She later became my maid of honor. She was a Greek girl, who also had just arrived in London for her studies in Law. I asked to borrow her laptop, as I did not have one of my own and tried to create my first CV. I thought that If I managed to secure a job, I would be able to sustain myself while I was studying.

I googled what a CV looks like and made a very basic copy of my own. I made a few printouts at the University copy center and began walking around the area in which the university campus was based, asking for a job. It didn't take me long to realize that even though I had graduated from a high school where English was the primary language, it would be difficult for me to converse with people who were native English speakers.

In addition, because Cyprus was not yet an EU member, I needed a work permit to be able work for anyone for more than 20 hours per week. The hourly rate for working students at the time was £4.25. Therefore, If I worked for all permitted hours, I would just about make £340 per month. It was not enough to live and study in London. I had thus decided to secure as many jobs as I could, in parallel to my studies, which would be willing to hire me over and above the 20 hours per week. I reached a stage where I was attending university 2-3 days per week and working for the rest.

I received a borderline first degree (a 2:1 eventually) when I graduated precisely 3 years later, while I also passed the test to become a Chartered Marketer of the Chartered Institute of Marketing in the UK. I was proud of myself. When you are determined, focused, and disciplined, along with having the appropriate support system such as family and friends around, hard work can pay off. I had gained enough confidence by that point to look for a full-time job in London and stay there for a little while. I successfully passed the Laiki Bank entrance tests in London, but I was unable to obtain a working visa. I had one more headache to cope with. I had to decide whether to pass up a fantastic job chance or figure out how to get a work permit in London. Well, as you can understand, securing a work permit was not feasible. I eventually gave in and accepted a position with a jewelry manufacturer that produced and exported a variety of jewelry to countries throughout the world, including Cyprus. I still have the Bank's job offer letter in my possession as a memento.

Although a university graduate, I was placed in the warehouse, along with unskilled staff, to prepare client orders. This translated into 8 hours of standing work, with 2 small breaks in-between. That job was not part of my career goals, nor my aspirations. It was, however, a great learning experience, as I got the opportunity to work with multiple cultures, in a setting which was tough. I was still young, just 20 years. I could pursue other roles that were in better alignment with my interests. I decided to move back to Cyprus and then and there the journey begins.

SECRET # 1

There will inevitably be moments in life when you face challenges that seem almost unbearable. Remember, these instances are not defined by the circumstances themselves, as everyone encounters difficulties at some point. Rather, it's your reaction to these situations that truly matters – your capacity to gracefully maneuver through obstacles.

It's important to recognize that your strength lies not in the events that unfold, but in how you choose to respond to them. Your actions in the face of adversity determine your true resilience. You possess the ability to master your thoughts and emotions, exercising control over your own mind, even when external circumstances appear overwhelming.

Remember, it's not the external world that wields power over you, but your inner fortitude that empowers you to shape your journey.

Ask yourself:

1. What is important to me?
2. Who inspires me and why?
3. What are the three things I do very well?

Ask your friends, family, and colleagues:

1. What are the three things that you would say I do very well?
2. Which five words would you use to describe me?
3. Would you hire me? If not, why not?

Often, we let fear hold us back from chasing our true desires, preventing us from even starting. Your fresh reality should spark excitement within you. Welcome challenges and new starts, for they lead to growth and bring you closer to where you truly fit. Remember this: Don't be afraid of closed doors. Embrace and learn from every difficulty you encounter. They arrive to teach you something valuable, propelling you forward.

Chapter 2

SKILL ENHANCEMENT AND EDUCATION

It wasn't until I had secured my second job, that I began getting a real grasp of the English language. Upon my return to Cyprus, back in 2005, I started emailing and faxing applications for work. A "marketing" job was typically a traveling sales role or one in which you were expected to sell advertising space in printed newspapers and magazines. What a disappointment!

My small island was too small for my big dreams. It took several weeks of calls and applications before I was able to get a job interview at a nearby academic institution that focused on tourism studies. I was overjoyed! When I learned that part of my job would involve traveling to Asian nations to recruit international students, I was even more excited. Needless to say, my parents were taken aback, as I was merely 22 years old. They thought that this would be too dangerous an endeavor for their little girl.

I would be making presentations in front of large school crowds for 15 days straight while traveling alone from city to city and promoting Cyprus as a study destination. There have been times when talking to anyone was hard for me. Even if I was just hungry, I was doing my best to connect by using hand gestures and a pocket dictionary that I was carrying. I recall rushing between airports in the middle of cities whose names I could not even pronounce while hauling heavy equipment. I also recall losing my flight, as none of the airport signage was in English.

There and then I decided that I had to learn the local language, as there was no other way for me to be able to get by.

By the time that my first trip was over, I was able to speak the basics in Chinese. I refused to eat cockroaches and other similar "treats" that were offered to me during my trips, but I was unable to resist the delicious fish and regional cooking that I was able to enjoy at small eateries that I would never have the opportunity to visit again in my life.

I will always be appreciative of having been given this chance at such a young age, despite the hardship of such journeys. These travels taught me how to be resilient, how to face obstacles head-on, how to discover answers when challenges seemed overwhelming, and last but not least, that life is a never-ending learning process.

Learning Chinese, using a map, adapting to different communication methods, polishing my body language reading abilities, developing my trust in others, and becoming comfortable outside of my comfort zone were all skills I had to acquire.

All was well, until we were no longer able to source students from Asia. Visas were denied by the local authorities, to reduce the number of "foreign" students entering the island. I had never in my life been fired, so that was a first.

I was at the time living with my father, in a small apartment that he had secured following my return from London. I was in charge of my own expenses (such as the car that I was using to get to work), as well as for food and school debt repayment.

The sudden loss of my job, an event entirely beyond my control, served as another imposing mountain that I was compelled to conquer.

I eventually learned that worries are just a state of mind, and ever since then, I've grown to not be afraid to move into the unknown.

Pure good fortune came my way at that precise moment. In less than two weeks, a recruiter who had been holding my resume since I had started looking for work called me. I had the chance to interview for a position with one of the Big Four Firms. I was in seventh heaven. I went to a total of three interviews, with members of the Board, before receiving the job offer.

I was committed to exerting every effort to demonstrate my best abilities and I did. Two years went by, and I came to realize that I didn't possess all the necessary job skills to succeed. My ambitions were lofty, but not quite grounded, as I can see now. It was then that I decided to pursue an MSc in Strategic Marketing. My research led me to discover that the only available Master's in science program, in my field of interest, was offered by an academic institution based in London.

Leaving my job and relocating to London was financially out of reach, yet foregoing the pursuit of a postgraduate degree was also not an option. I faced a crucial choice that required bold action. I opted to retain my job, using the income to support my MSc studies, and committed to commuting to London on a weekly basis for the upcoming two years. I cannot deny that it was exhausting and very costly.

During that period, Fridays meant a half day at work. So, I would catch the late afternoon flight with British or Cyprus Airways to London, arriving by nightfall. Following that, I'd wait at the bus stop, board a two-hour bus route to Hertfordshire, and reach the hostel well into Friday night. On both Saturday and Sunday, I dedicated myself to 8-hour classes. Finally, on Sunday at 10pm, I'd take the return flight to

Larnaca Airport, ensuring I was back in time to start work at 8am on Monday.

Amidst this demanding schedule, I had to tackle coursework and take exams. The culmination of my efforts arrived 1.5 years later, as I proudly graduated with a Distinction.

I could have opted for inertia – the path of mere survival – by shying away from acquiring new skills and contenting myself with my existing abilities, all while staying in my current job. However, I recognized that this would eventually lead to being outshone by more capable peers. Instead, I embraced the challenging route, driven by my steadfast conviction that the correct path is often the more demanding one.

SECRET # 2

Learning is a timeless thread woven through every part of life, showing us that we can keep gaining knowledge at any age. The idea that it's never too late to learn new things shows how limitless our potential is. Time patiently waits for us to begin, guiding us as we explore new things. The past doesn't trap us; it gives us a canvas to pursue our dreams. Just like the sun rises each day, we can awaken our passions, learn new skills, and discover new ideas.

Whether we're at the end of our careers or just starting out, learning is a journey of self-discovery and change. When we approach something new, it's not a wall but a bridge to opportunity. Many success stories remind us that learning continues, and we all have our unique contributions to make, no matter where we are in life.

These are my top ten tips:

1. **Set Clear Goals:** Setting specific, achievable goals will guide your skill enhancement efforts and help you stay motivated.
2. **Continuous Learning:** Embrace a growth mindset and commit to lifelong learning. The world is constantly evolving, and staying up to date with new knowledge and skills is crucial.
3. **Choose Relevant Skills:** Focus on skills that align with your interests, strengths, and the demands of your chosen field. Prioritize skills that will enhance your career prospects.
4. **Effective Time Management:** Allocate dedicated time for learning and skill development. Create a schedule that balances your educational pursuits with other responsibilities.
5. **Utilize Online Resources:** Take advantage of online courses, tutorials, webinars, and educational platforms. The

internet offers a wealth of resources to help you acquire new skills.

6. **Practice and Application:** Apply what you learn through hands-on projects, real-world scenarios, or practical exercises. Active application reinforces your understanding and skill proficiency.

7. **Networking and Collaboration:** Engage with peers, mentors, and professionals in your field. Networking can provide insights, opportunities, and potential collaborations for skill enhancement.

8. **Receive Constructive Feedback:** Seek feedback from experts or peers to identify areas for improvement. Constructive criticism can accelerate your skill development by addressing blind spots.

9. **Reflect and Iterate**: Regularly evaluate your progress and adjust your learning strategies as needed. Reflect on what's working and what isn't and be willing to adapt your approach.

10. **Balance Theory and Practice:** Combine theoretical knowledge with hands-on experience. Practical application of skills reinforces theoretical concepts and enhances your overall competence.

I must admit that the key to successful skill enhancement and education is dedication, perseverance, and a willingness to adapt and grow. Your efforts in continuous learning will contribute significantly to your personal and professional development.

Chapter 3

AN IMPRESSIVE RESUME AND COVER LETTER

After wrapping up my MSc, an additional year elapsed during which I continued in the same job position at the esteemed Big Four Firm. A sense of stagnation began to take hold, and as I've acknowledged before, the prospect of stagnancy is what I dread most.

Driven by a thirst for fresh challenges, I embarked on a journey of initiating endeavors that could steer me towards new horizons. I made the decision to draft a strong CV and an appealing cover letter, and I started submitting applications for lecturing and training positions at local universities with the intention of engaging in teaching activities outside of my usual job hours. It worked! At the same time, I was assigned to hold part of the orientation training that the Big Four firm offered to newly contracted staff. It was then that I identified a strong professional inclination aligned with my core strengths and interests, that of training other people.

Not long after, I made the decision to resign from my job and embark on an entrepreneurial journey. With a lineage rooted in self-made entrepreneurs, it felt like my inherent calling was speaking to me.

I presented the idea of maintaining an outsourced supplier relationship to my former employer, a partnership that lasted for the subsequent five years. Following this successful arrangement, I formally resigned and proceeded to secure my first tiny office space on a rental basis.

The core focus of my initial business encompassed outsourced marketing services. In this capacity, we functioned as the dedicated marketing team for small to medium-sized enterprises, meticulously implementing their strategies and plans on a monthly retainer basis. The company grew to employing 7 people and serving some of the most well-known brands. Around that time, I had personally created a very strong network of contacts, who were asking for personal career advice.

A significant portion of these individuals were actively seeking new career opportunities, pursuing promotions, or contemplating a career transition. They approached me with inquiries regarding crafting more compelling resumes and bolstering their online presence. While my expertise held relevance, it wasn't exclusively centered on that aspect.

Recognizing this, I believed it was time to broaden and enhance my skill set and knowledge. Subsequently, I enrolled in a highly specialized Certification course, orchestrated by none other than the President of the International Association of Image Makers, scheduled to take place in London. The course spanned two sessions, each extending over two weeks, with the instructor making the journey from the U.S.

Notably, participants converged from diverse corners, including places as distant as Mexico and Hong Kong. The investment that was required was substantial, nonetheless, I had complete confidence that the investment would be entirely worthwhile. The curriculum included everything about building and communicating a compelling personal brand, online and offline, as well as self-marketing and employability skills.

Truthfully, that course proved to be the most beneficial and impactful one I had undertaken up until that point in my life.

Upon its conclusion, I transitioned to establish yet another business, centered solely on providing training and consulting services to individuals and groups.

This structure afforded me the opportunity to forge close partnerships with CEOs, government officials, prospective parliamentarians, chosen mayors, and individuals from diverse backgrounds, as well as regular people like you and me. In this capacity, I aided them in refining their attire and communication, crafting impactful speeches, mastering public speaking, composing persuasive resumes and cover letters, and excelling in interviews while skillfully negotiating their packages.

SECRET # 3

It's important to recognize that a one-size-fits-all approach simply doesn't suffice. A generic, off-the-shelf resume lacks the ability to resonate with every individual. Employers are genuinely interested in gaining insight into your identity from the resume you've shared. They're seeking a genuine representation, not another dull copy-and-paste composition.

Your resume is a snapshot of your professional life and should make a strong first impression. Tailor it to showcase your strengths and demonstrate why you're the ideal candidate for the job.

Here are some tips to help you craft a standout Resume:

1. **Tailor for the Job**: Customize your resume for each job application. Highlight skills and experiences that directly relate to the specific job requirements. Use keywords from the job description to demonstrate your fit for the role.

2. **Clear Structure and Format**:

   a. Choose a clean, professional font.
   b. Use bullet points for easy readability.
   c. Organize your content with clear headings (e.g., "Summary," "Experience," "Education," etc.).
   d. Maintain a consistent format throughout.

3. **Contact Information**:

   a. Include your full name, phone number, email address, and location.
   b. LinkedIn profile: If you have one, include a link to your LinkedIn profile, which can provide more context about your professional background.

4. **Professional Summary/Objective**:

a. Write a concise, compelling summary at the top of your resume that highlights your key skills, experience, and what you bring to the table.
b. If you include an objective, make it specific to the job you're applying for.

5. **Work Experience**:

a. List your work experience in reverse chronological order (most recent job first).
b. For each position, include the company name, your job title, the dates of employment, and a brief description of your responsibilities and accomplishments.
c. Use action verbs to start each bullet point (e.g., "Managed," "Achieved," "Collaborated").
d. Quantify your achievements wherever possible (e.g., "Increased sales by 25%," "Managed a team of 10 employees").

6. **Skills and Qualifications**:

a. Include a dedicated section for relevant skills, both technical and soft skills.
b. Tailor this section to match the job requirements.

7. **Education**:

a. List your educational background, including the name of the institution, degree earned, graduation date, and any relevant honors.
b. Include any certifications, workshops, or additional training that is pertinent to the job.

8. **Achievements and Awards**: Highlight any notable achievements, awards, or recognition you've received in your career.

9. **Proofreading and Editing**:

   a. Ensure your resume is free of grammatical and spelling errors.
   b. Ask a friend or mentor to review your resume for feedback.

10. **Length**: Keep your resume concise, ideally limited to one page for less experienced candidates and up to two pages for those with extensive experience.

11. **Visual Appeal**: Use subtle design elements (e.g., bold headings, a touch of color) to make your resume visually appealing but avoid overdoing it.

At the same time, the same amount of attention should be given to creating your cover letter as it is your opportunity to showcase your enthusiasm, qualifications, and fitness for the role. It should engage the reader and make them want to learn more about you through an interview.

Writing a compelling cover letter is essential for making a strong first impression on potential employers. Here are some tips to help you craft an effective cover letter:

1. **Customize for Each Job**: Tailor your cover letter to the specific job you're applying for. Highlight relevant skills, experiences, and qualifications that match the job description.

2. **Format and Structure**:

   a. Use a professional format: Your cover letter should be well-organized and easy to read.
   b. Address it properly: If possible, address the letter to a

specific person. If not, use a generic greeting like "Dear Hiring Manager."

c. Keep it concise: Aim for around 3-4 paragraphs and try to keep the letter within one page.

3. **Opening Paragraph**:

a. Grab their attention: Start with a strong opening sentence that captures the reader's interest.

b. Mention the position: State the position you're applying for and how you learned about it.

c. Briefly introduce yourself: Provide a concise overview of your background and why you're interested in the role.

4. **Middle Paragraph(s)**:

a. Highlight your qualifications: Focus on specific skills and experiences that make you a strong fit for the job. Use examples to demonstrate your abilities.

b. Connect with the company: Show that you've researched the company by mentioning something you admire about their work, values, or recent achievements.

5. **Closing Paragraph**:

a. Express enthusiasm: Reiterate your interest in the position and your desire to contribute to the company's success.

b. Mention next steps: Politely indicate that you're looking forward to the opportunity for an interview or further discussion.

6. **Language and Tone**:

    a. Be professional: Use formal language and avoid slang or overly casual expressions.
    b. Showcase your personality: While maintaining professionalism, infuse your cover letter with your unique voice and personality.
    c. Use action verbs: Start sentences with strong action verbs to convey confidence and impact.

7. **Proofread and Edit**:

    a. Check for errors: Thoroughly proofread your cover letter for grammar, spelling, and punctuation mistakes.
    b. Consistency: Ensure that your cover letter aligns with your resume and other application materials.

8. **Show, Don't Just Tell**: Provide specific examples: Instead of making general claims, use specific instances where you demonstrated relevant skills or achievements.

9. **Quantify Achievements**: Whenever possible, use numbers to quantify your accomplishments. This adds credibility to your claims.

10. **Avoid Repeating Your Resume**: Your cover letter should complement your resume, not duplicate it. Focus on aspects that can't be captured in your resume.

11. **Be Honest and Authentic**: Highlight your strengths but be truthful about your experiences and abilities. Authenticity is key.

12. **Use a Professional Closing**: Sign off with a polite and professional closing, such as "Sincerely" or "Best regards," followed by your name.

Chapter 4

NETWORKING AND PERSONAL BRANDING

To maintain a thriving business venture and cover the expenses of employee salaries, I recognized the necessity of broadening my professional network. This realization prompted me to take a significant step – I established a presence on LinkedIn, inspired by a client's comment. This was my first foray into the world of online business networking.

LinkedIn was still relatively unfamiliar at the time. In fact, during that very week, I received an invitation to give a public speech at the University of Cyprus, addressing approximately 150 students. When I inquired how many of them were using LinkedIn, only a small fraction, about 10%, raised their hands. Naturally, I had been registered on Facebook and Twitter for quite some time, but these platforms aren't commonly utilized for broadening one's professional connections.

Admittedly, social media has the potential to effectively assist in cultivating a robust personal brand, provided that each account is carefully created and expertly managed and they all communicate the same message about you.

That being said, I want to emphasize that regardless of the extent of your online network, the influence of in-person business networking far surpasses the impact of online platforms.

Making myself available to give complementary keynotes, public speeches, and motivational presentations to universities, government organizations, and social groups, was one way through which I grew my in-person business network and developed a strong personal brand.

It was during one of these impactful speeches that I had the privilege of crossing paths with the woman who would later become my invaluable mentor. Her guidance paved the way for my inclusion among a select community of accomplished and distinguished female entrepreneurs and I was only still in my late 20's. She saw the burning passion and brilliant enthusiasm in my eyes, which made her realize that my objectives had my whole heart.

I was honored to receive a nomination from the European Commission to serve as an ambassador for the European Network of Female Entrepreneurship Ambassadors. This esteemed role afforded me the opportunity to attend conferences across Europe, fully supported by the European Commission, where I engaged with a diverse group of accomplished Female Entrepreneurs.

These networking events provided a platform for meaningful exchanges of ideas and experiences, even as I found myself in the company of entrepreneurs often possessing double my years of wisdom. Together, we collaborated to nurture and enhance our respective businesses. A multitude of opportunities unfolded throughout Europe, and with each passing moment, my network continued to flourish. A significant responsibility entrusted to me was the task of imparting training to women in remote and rural locations, such as the outskirts of Tbilisi, Georgia.

Before long, the reach of my personal brand extended even to the State Department of the United States Embassy in Cyprus. It was one morning like any other when my phone rang, and I answered an unexpected yet momentous call. An Embassy officer presented me with a remarkable proposition. She inquired if I would consider joining a prestigious assembly of Global Female Leaders.

This distinguished cohort would embark on a 21-day journey across various states within the U.S., and the entire experience, including expenses, would be graciously covered.

In a role of national representation, I would stand alongside a select gathering of 100 distinguished global female leaders. This esteemed assembly offered an exclusive opportunity to engage with prominent figures on the world stage, including personalities like Hillary Clinton and Michelle Obama. The itinerary encompassed not only these inspiring encounters but also immersive workshops and visits to prominent corporate entities, among them Deloitte and EY New York.

SECRET # 4

Even if digital communication has grown in popularity recently, face-to-face encounters still have many advantages, particularly when it comes to networking. The benefits of in-person business networking include the following:

1. **Establishing Genuine Connections:** In-person interactions allow you to establish more genuine and authentic connections with others. Meeting someone face-to-face helps build trust and rapport more effectively than online communication, as you can read body language, facial expressions, and other nonverbal cues.

2. **Unforeseen Encounters:** In-person events, seminars, conferences, and networking gatherings offer opportunities for unanticipated encounters with people you might not have otherwise met. These chance interactions can lead to job offers, valuable collaborations, partnerships, or business opportunities.

3. **Credibility and Professionalism:** Participating in face-to-face networking events can enhance your credibility and professionalism. It shows that you are actively engaged in your industry and committed to offering value to a future employer, as well as building meaningful relationships.

4. **Feedback and Learning:** In-person networking offers a dynamic platform for receiving instant feedback, continuous learning, and the potential for discovering job offers. By actively participating in dialogues with both peers and seasoned industry professionals, you can acquire valuable insights, foster idea exchange, and gain direct exposure to emerging opportunities on the horizon.

5. **Personal Branding:** In-person networking enables you to present your personal brand through your appearance, communication approach, and engagements. This actively

shapes the way you're perceived within your field, ensuring that you're top-of-mind when an opportunity presents itself.

6. **Local and Global Connections:** Although digital communication facilitates global connections and proves beneficial when seeking remote job opportunities, the potency of face-to-face networking lies in its ability to forge strong local bonds. These connections within your vicinity can pave the way for referrals, partnerships, and collaborations that hold geographical significance.

Face-to-face business networking provides a unique and valuable opportunity to establish meaningful connections, foster trust, and enhance your professional presence. While online networking has its advantages, in-person interactions offer a depth of communication and relationship-building that can be difficult to replicate through digital means.

Chapter 5

JOB SEARCH STRATEGIES

Everything was thriving; I was consistently honing my skills while witnessing the impressive growth of my ventures. Reflecting on Nelson Mandela's wisdom, "Do not judge me by my success, judge me by how many times I fell down and got back up again". I found his words resonating deeply. Once more, the narrative of life unfolded, with history seemingly repeating its steps.

I once again found myself dealing with the difficulties of a recession and the fallout from our country's famed policies, such a haircut and strict capital controls. In addition to the frustrating problem of having no access to cash, another setback occurred when our annual customer contracts, which had been meticulously secured over time, were abruptly cancelled in not more than 10 days. Rock bottom became the solid foundation in which I had to rebuild my life, as J.K. Rowling said also.

Any remaining funds had to be allocated towards fulfilling commitments to government authorities and covering both salaries and the inevitable task of letting go of every staff member. A glimmer of hope for imminent recovery seemed elusive. Our services consistently played a secondary role for both corporations and individuals, viewed more as a luxury than a necessity. Priorities were distinctly clear, demanding attention to crucial matters like payroll, financial record-keeping, and legal obligations.

The businesses were in their infancy, and I too was navigating the unfamiliar terrain of the business world. A lack of contingency plans further exacerbated the situation. What I can share with you is this: Embrace risks—when you succeed, happiness awaits; when you fail, wisdom is your reward.

I had to start looking for a job because there was no other choice. It was tough due to the bad job market and the challenge of going from a boss to an employee, which I had to accept.

How could I find a job that aligned so perfectly with my passions that I would experience the truth of Confucius' words – "Choose a job you love, and you will never have to work a day in your life"? I recall coming across a quote saying that you need to "Start where you are. Use what you have. Do what you can" and I did.

It didn't take long for me to come to the realization that the economy was in such a dire state that hardly any job openings were being advertised during that period. Despite my persistent efforts, I found myself having dispatched more than 150 resumes, yet not a single response came my way.

I had taken the proactive step of configuring job alerts to keep me informed about pertinent job openings. However, it became increasingly apparent that none of these alerts aligned with my academic qualifications and professional experience.

With few alternatives left, I embarked on my final recourse. I began reaching out to both acquaintances and strangers, fervently inquiring about potential job opportunities. This involved sending direct emails to CEOs of companies, ranging from small enterprises to medium-sized firms to large corporations, all in an earnest attempt to secure employment. I had to do what I had to do.

My new life would cost me my old one. It would cost me my comfort zone and my sense of direction. It would cost me being liked and understood, but it didn't matter. After experiencing more than a year of unemployment, I found myself in a unique position to welcome my first daughter into the world. Subsequently, I secured a role with reduced hours and responsibilities at an esteemed Academic Institution.

As a semblance of stability started to take hold once more, a sense of restlessness began to creep in. In response, I resolved to confront this unease head-on by embarking on the journey to become a Certified Soft-Skills Trainer, a pursuit facilitated by the local Human Resource Development Authority.

Successively, I gained the capacity to deliver structured corporate training, enabling my clients to avail government funding for every training session they arranged within their organizational confines.

By diversifying my income streams through pursuits aligned with my passion, I not only embraced what I loved but also fortified my ability to provide for my family and attain a heightened level of financial stability.

SECRET # 5

Job searching can be a challenging process, but with the right strategies, you can increase your chances of finding a job that fits your skills and goals. Here are some effective job search strategies:

1. **Set Clear Goals**: Define your job search goals, such as the type of job, industry, salary range, and location you're targeting. Having clear goals will help you focus your efforts.

2. **Online Job Boards**: Utilize job search websites and platforms like LinkedIn Jobs, and company websites to search for job openings. Set up job alerts to receive notifications for relevant positions.

3. **Company Research**: Research companies that align with your values and interests. Learn about their culture, mission, recent news, and job openings. This knowledge will be valuable during interviews and networking conversations.

4. **Informational Interviews**: Reach out to professionals in your desired field for informational interviews. These conversations can provide insights into the industry, company, and potential job opportunities.

5. **Temporary and Freelance Work**: Consider taking temporary or freelance assignments to gain experience, expand your network, and potentially transition into a full-time role.

6. **Cold Outreach**: If you're interested in a specific company, reach out directly to inquire about job openings or express your interest in working for them.

7. **Job Fairs and Career Events**: Attend job fairs, career expos, and industry-specific events to meet recruiters and learn about job opportunities.

8. **Recruitment Agencies**: Register with recruitment agencies or staffing firms that specialize in your field. They can help match you with suitable job openings.

9. **Follow Up**: After submitting applications or attending interviews, send a follow-up email to express your continued interest and gratitude for the opportunity.

10. **Stay Organized:** Keep track of the jobs you've applied for, interviews you've attended, and follow-ups you've sent. This organization will help you manage your job search effectively.

Job searching can take time, so be patient and persistent. Adjust your strategies based on your experiences and results, and don't hesitate to seek advice from career counselors or mentors.

Chapter 6

INTERVIEW PREPARATION

A couple of years down the road I found myself at a crossroad in my career. An opportunity to interview with a tech company I had long admired presented itself. The role they were offering seemed tailor-made for my skills and aligned perfectly with my interests. I was determined to make a great impression.

As I began my interview preparation, I dove deep into researching the company's services and recent developments. I wanted to understand not only what they did but also their company culture and values. Conducting this thorough research played a pivotal role in shaping my approach to the interview. It allowed me to strategically customize my responses, effectively showcasing my authentic enthusiasm for becoming an integral member of their team in the role of Marketing Manager.

I also spent a significant amount of time practicing my responses to common interview questions. I wrote down specific examples from my previous work experiences that demonstrated my skills and abilities. I practiced speaking confidently about these examples to ensure I could articulate my accomplishments clearly during the interview.

One aspect of interview preparation that I found particularly helpful was conducting mock interviews with my husband. He posed challenging questions, critiqued my answers, and provided valuable feedback on my body language and communication style. These practice sessions helped me refine my responses and build my confidence.

On the day of the interview, I made sure to arrive early, dressed in professional attire. I had printed copies of my resume, cover letter, and a list of questions I wanted to ask the interviewers.

Having physical copies made me feel more prepared and organized.

During the interview itself, which was eventually held by the company's CTO, I focused on maintaining good eye contact, using confident body language, and actively listening to his questions. I drew on the examples I had prepared and adapted them to the specific questions asked. Whenever I encountered a question that I hadn't anticipated, I took a moment to gather my thoughts before responding thoughtfully.

After progressing through a series of three interviews, I received the gratifying news that I had been selected for the position. However, the excitement didn't stop there. To my pleasant surprise, the offer extended to me was even more remarkable—an elevated role as Marketing Director, a testament to the potential and value I had demonstrated throughout the interview process.

In the lead-up to receiving this offer, I encountered a series of rejections from positions I had applied for. In retrospect, these setbacks were likely a result of insufficiently tailored preparation and the challenge of managing stress effectively.

While I didn't end up getting every job for which I applied, the experience taught me the importance of thorough interview preparation and the value of adapting to unexpected situations. It also reminded me that every interview is a chance to learn and improve for the next opportunity. Ultimately, the effort I put into preparing for each one of those interviews paid off in subsequent interviews and helped me land a role that was an even better fit for my skills and aspirations. It reinforced the idea that interview preparation isn't just about impressing the interviewers; it's about demonstrating your genuine interest, showcasing your abilities, and presenting your best self.

SECRET # 6

Failing to prepare is preparation to fail that interview. Here are some tips to help you prepare effectively:

1. **Understand the Role:** Review the job description and requirements thoroughly. Identify the key responsibilities and skills needed for the position. Be ready to discuss how your experience matches these requirements.

2. **Practice Common Interview Questions:** Prepare answers for common questions like "Tell me about yourself," "Why do you want to work here?" and "What are your strengths/weaknesses?" Practice your responses to ensure they're clear, concise, and highlight your relevant experience.

3. **Behavioral Examples:** Prepare specific examples from your past experiences that demonstrate your skills, problem-solving abilities, teamwork, and leadership. Use the STAR (Situation, Task, Action, Result) method to structure your answers.

4. **Tailor Your Resume:** Review your resume and be ready to discuss the experiences and achievements listed. Connect them to the job requirements and highlight how they make you a strong fit for the role.

5. **Develop Questions:** Prepare thoughtful questions to ask the interviewer about the company, team dynamics, expectations, and growth opportunities. Asking questions demonstrates your interest and engagement.

6. **Plan Your Journey:** Know the interview location and consider traffic or transportation options. Arrive a bit early to account for any unforeseen delays.

7. **First Impressions**: Your appearance is the first thing the interviewer notices about you. Dressing appropriately shows that you value the opportunity and have taken the time to prepare for the interview.

8. **Practice Good Body Language:** Maintain eye contact, offer a firm handshake, and sit up straight. Use open and engaged body language to convey confidence and interest.

9. **Manage Nervousness:** Practice deep breathing or relaxation techniques to calm your nerves before the interview. Remember that it's okay to feel a bit nervous—it's natural!

10. **Mock Interviews:** Practice with a friend, family member, or career coach. Mock interviews can help you refine your answers, receive feedback, and become more comfortable with the interview format.

11. **Review Your Online Presence:** Ensure your social media profiles are professional and clean. Employers often check online presence as part of the hiring process.

12. **Adapt to the Digital Age:** Showcase your proficiency in digital skills and your capacity to excel in a technology-centric professional landscape. Embrace the potential for remote work opportunities and proactively equip yourself for virtual interviews.

I can assure you that preparation is key to performing well in an interview. The more you practice and research, the more confident and capable you'll feel during the actual interview.

Good luck!

Chapter 7

FOLLOW UP AND THANK YOU NOTES

On a bright and sunlit weekday, the melodious ring of my phone broke the silence. With a sense of interest, I answered, greeted by the voice of a lady representing one of the prestigious International Professional Services Firms. She explained that my resume had caught her attention from a previous submission, and she inquired whether I would be open to participating in an interview for a Senior Management position. I found myself in a nerve-wracking yet exciting position – could this be my chance to embark on a journey with such a distinguished firm?

Despite my lack of confidence, I would do everything in my power to leave a positive impression. After a successful interview that left me feeling both exhilarated and slightly anxious, I knew I had to take additional steps to stand out.

As soon as I returned home from the interview, I sat down at my computer and started crafting individualized thank-you emails for each member of the interview panel. I wanted my gratitude to shine through, so I made sure to mention specific aspects of our conversation that resonated with me. I also expressed my enthusiasm for the company's culture and the projects they were working on. These notes weren't just about following up; they were a genuine extension of my appreciation and interest in the role.

A few days later, I received an email from one of the interviewers – the head of the department I would potentially be working in. He expressed his gratitude for the thank-you note and mentioned how it had sparked further discussions among the team about my potential fit for the role. The email not only validated my approach but also gave me a glimmer of hope in the midst of the waiting period. In the following weeks, I continued to stay engaged. I shared relevant industry articles and insights that I thought would be valuable to the team. These interactions weren't forced; they stemmed from my genuine passion for the field and my eagerness to contribute even before potentially joining the company.

After what felt like an eternity of anticipation, the phone finally rang one day. It was the hiring manager, and she had fantastic news. I had been selected for the position, and they were excited to have me on board.

The hiring manager mentioned how my consistent follow-up and thoughtful engagement had set me apart from other candidates. She appreciated my genuine interest and proactive approach, which aligned perfectly with the company's values.

As I embarked on my journey with the Firm, I carried this valuable lesson with me – that the effort I put into following up and sending thank-you notes wasn't just a formality; it was an opportunity to showcase my dedication, enthusiasm, and professionalism.

It transformed a simple interview into a meaningful connection that opened doors to an exciting new chapter in my career.

SECRET # 7

Sending follow-up and thank you notes after a job interview is a crucial step in the hiring process. It shows your professionalism, enthusiasm, and appreciation for the opportunity. Here are some tips for crafting effective follow-up and thank you notes:

1. **Be Prompt:** Send your follow-up and thank you notes within 24 hours of the interview to demonstrate your eagerness and attention to detail.
2. **Personalize Each Note:** Customize your messages for each interviewer. Mention specific topics you discussed or aspects of the interview that stood out to make your notes more personalized and memorable.
3. **Express Gratitude:** Begin your note by expressing sincere gratitude for the opportunity to interview and for the time the interviewer(s) spent with you.
4. **Reiterate Interest:** Reiterate your interest in the position and the company. Highlight the reasons why you're excited about the role and how your skills align with their needs.
5. **Mention Key Points:** Briefly touch upon key points discussed during the interview, such as your qualifications, relevant experiences, and any unique insights you gained about the company.
6. **Address Concerns:** If there were any areas where you felt you didn't fully address a question or want to clarify something, you can do so in your thank you note.
7. **Show Enthusiasm:** Express enthusiasm for the opportunity to contribute to the company's success and mention how you're looking forward to potentially joining their team.
8. **Professional Tone:** Keep your tone professional, polite, and positive throughout the note. Avoid using slang or overly casual language.

9. **Proofread:** Ensure your note is free of grammatical and spelling errors. A well-written note reflects attention to detail and professionalism.

10. **Use Email:** In most cases, email is the preferred method of communication for follow-up and thank you notes. It's quick and allows you to easily attach any additional materials if necessary.

Sending follow-up and thank you notes is not only a courteous gesture but also an opportunity to leave a lasting positive impression on the interviewers. Take the time to craft thoughtful and personalized messages that reflect your genuine interest and enthusiasm for the position.

Chapter 8

NEGOTIATING JOB OFFERS

I was thrilled about the opportunity of becoming a Senior Manager at a prestigious Global Firm, but I knew that the initial offer they presented wasn't quite aligned with my expectations and market value.

Instead of immediately accepting the offer, I decided to negotiate. I did my research to understand the average salary range for similar roles in the industry and location, as well as the company's financial health and funding status. Armed with this information, I crafted a polite and professional email to the hiring manager, expressing my gratitude for the offer and explaining why I believed I deserved a higher salary based on my skills, experience, and the market value.

I emphasized how my background could bring unique value to the team and highlighted some specific accomplishments that showcased my expertise. I also mentioned that I was genuinely excited about joining the company and contributing to its growth.

The hiring manager responded positively, acknowledging my points, and expressing appreciation for my enthusiasm. They mentioned that they were willing to revisit the salary offer and asked me for a specific figure that I had in mind. I replied with a slightly higher but reasonable number, while also mentioning that I was open to discussing other compensation components such as a pension fund, mileage coverage, remote work, or additional benefits. As a dedicated working mother, I truly valued the opportunity to discuss the possibility of additional flexibility, a topic that had been brought up during our ongoing negotiation conversations. There was a brief back-and-forth as we worked to find a mutually agreeable compensation package. The company eventually came back with a revised offer that was closer to my expectations, and we were able to finalize the details.

Throughout the negotiation process, I maintained a respectful and collaborative tone. I made sure to convey my excitement about the role and the company while also advocating for my own interests. In the end, I felt that the negotiation helped set a positive tone for my future relationship with the company, as it showed that I was proactive, confident, and invested in my own career growth.

The experience taught me that negotiation is a normal and expected part of the job offer process. It's important to be prepared, do your research, and approach the conversation with professionalism and positivity.

SECRET # 8

Negotiating a job offer can be a crucial step in securing a favorable compensation package and overall employment terms. Here are some tips to help you navigate the negotiation process effectively:

1. **Do Your Research**: Before entering negotiations, research the industry standard for the position you're applying for. Websites like Glassdoor, Payscale, and industry-specific salary surveys can provide valuable insights into average compensation for similar roles in your region.

2. **Understand Your Value**: Consider your skills, experience, education, and unique qualities that make you an asset to the company. Highlight how your qualifications align with the responsibilities of the role and contribute to the company's success.

3. **Timing is Key**: Wait for the employer to make the first offer. This allows you to gather information and understand their initial evaluation of your skills. If you're asked about your salary expectations, you can provide a range based on your research.

4. **Negotiate More Than Just Salary**: While salary is important, don't forget to negotiate other aspects of the package, such as bonuses, health benefits, retirement plans, flexible work arrangements, remote work possibilities, professional development opportunities, and more.

5. **Prioritize Your Must-Haves**: Identify the aspects of the offer that are non-negotiable for you. Focus on negotiating these first before moving on to other elements.

6. **Practice Effective Communication**: Maintain a professional and positive tone throughout the negotiation process. Clearly articulate your points and be prepared to explain how your skills and experience justify your requests.

7. **Be Flexible**: While it's important to advocate for your needs, be willing to compromise and find a middle ground that benefits both you and the employer.

8. **Stay Patient and Calm**: Negotiations may take time, and it's possible that the process may involve multiple rounds of discussions. Stay patient and avoid rushing into decisions.

9. **Use Objective Criteria**: When negotiating, support your requests with objective data and specific reasons. For example, mention how your past achievements directly contributed to your previous employer's growth or how your skills will benefit the new company.

10. **Get Offers in Writing**: Once you reach an agreement, make sure to get the final offer in writing before formally accepting the position.

Negotiation is a skill that improves with practice. Don't be afraid to ask for what you're worth and to negotiate for a package that aligns with your needs and expectations.

Chapter 9

ACCEPTANCE AND ONBOARDING

One of the most remarkable employment experiences I've had was during my tenure as the Leader of Ronald McDonald House Charities® in Cyprus. When I was first appointed, my task was to establish the inaugural Ronald McDonald House on the island. The core mission of the Ronald McDonald House is to extend a comforting "home away from home" to families, enabling them to remain close to their child's medical facility while receiving invaluable emotional and practical assistance during the trying moments they face. The scale of this undertaking was immense, compounded by the urgency to secure necessary funds within an exceptionally short timeframe, a challenge intensified by the COVID-19 pandemic and the widespread lockdown measures that prevailed at the time.

I was interviewed and offered the position by an exceptional man, who was then serving as the Board Chair of the Charity. The organization's scope may vary between different chapters and locations, but the overarching goal remains the same: to provide comfort, care, and assistance to families in need. I felt a deep sense of honor upon being selected. This role entailed the responsibility of heading, staffing, overseeing, and nurturing the local chapter of a global philanthropic institution dedicated to creating a supportive and nurturing haven for families with seriously ill or injured children undergoing medical treatment at nearby hospitals.

For the first time, I embraced the offer wholeheartedly, skipping the customary background checks. I recognized that my mission held a greater significance than my individual needs and expectations. This role would give me a once in a lifetime opportunity to give back to the community, to the people in need. However, this does not imply that I bypassed the crucial step of immersing myself entirely in the organization's worldwide culture, operational methods, and anticipated standards. Fortunately, I had the privilege of being guided by a mentor, friend, and colleague stationed in Chicago, U.S. Their role was that of a regional field manager, entrusted with ensuring the comprehensive implementation of global directives.

I want to highlight that in today's interconnected and competitive business world, comprehending your organization's culture, operations, and expected standards is incredibly vital. This knowledge improves communication, simplifies teamwork, and boosts the flexibility of decision-making.

Adhering to standards guarantees quality, and cultural sensitivity fosters respect and teamwork. Ultimately, embracing these aspects nurtures a unified global perspective that drives both personal growth within the company and the company's long-term success.

SECRET # 9

An important choice that could have a long-lasting effect on your career and personal life is accepting a job offer. No offer should be accepted hastily without adequate time to consider it from all sides. Before deciding what to do next, I would suggest that you carry out the following steps:

1. Review the Job Offer Thoroughly:

In order to make an informed choice, it is crucial to take the time to carefully analyze the employment offer. This phase enables you to comprehend the conditions of employment, such as pay, benefits, job duties, and any contractual obligations. You can prevent further misunderstandings and problems by thoroughly reading the offer. It also enables you to determine whether the position fits with your values, talents, and career objectives.

2. Paperwork and Background Checks:

Starting a new job requires administrative chores that may appear boring, but they are essential for organizational and legal reasons. You may be confident that you're officially on board and qualified for the company's benefits by completing documentation, including employment contracts, tax filings, and benefits enrollment. Background checks are frequently performed to confirm your credentials and guarantee a secure and reliable work environment. You show your dedication to the position and the organization's compliance standards by swiftly fulfilling these obligations.

3. Familiarize Yourself:

Familiarizing yourself with the company culture and expectations before your start date can give you a head start in acclimating to your new environment. Learning about the company's values, mission, and working norms helps you understand what's important to the organization and how you can contribute effectively. This knowledge can also guide your interactions with colleagues, supervisors, and clients, making your transition smoother.

Moreover, understanding expectations helps you align your skills and performance with what's required, setting you up for success from day one.

In summary, these steps collectively contribute to a successful onboarding experience and long-term satisfaction in your new job. Taking the time to review the offer, complete paperwork, and learn about the company culture demonstrates your professionalism, dedication, and willingness to integrate seamlessly into the team. By approaching these steps with careful consideration, you set the stage for a positive and productive journey in your new role.

Chapter 10

BELIEVE YOU CAN AND YOU ARE HALFWAY THERE

We've reached the concluding chapter, and it holds a special place in my heart. This is the part I cherish the most in this book, as it allows me to convey a powerful message: You possess the remarkable capacity to chase after your every aspiration. Always remember to carry your confidence with you on your journey, wherever life takes you.

The human mind has the ability to shape and influence various aspects of our lives, including our actions, emotions, perceptions, and even our external circumstances. Thoughts are the mental processes that involve the conscious and subconscious mind, encompassing ideas, beliefs, attitudes, and perceptions. Your thoughts are in your total control. They can either propel you toward success or hold you back.

One might assume that my words stem from a place of comfort. However, I can assure you that whenever I approach the vicinity of a comfort zone, I swiftly step out and embark on a quest for my next challenge. This mirrors my approach to writing this very book, while on my summer vacation from work and babysitting my two young children.

I've never let anything, or anyone get in the way of my decisions. Although there have been instances where my choices weren't optimal, I've been willing to embrace those moments. Taking full ownership of my mistakes, I've found comfort in the process of learning and growing from them. My memories of the time I hired a colleague as an executive coach to help me navigate a crucial period in my career are still very clear. This was the turning point where I boldly decided to quit my previous career and forge forth into the unexplored territory of fully devoting myself to my dream job. This goal included coaching, consulting, and training others—a task that was firmly in line with my inner calling.

Even though my heart yearned for this path, I struggled with doubt. Given my obligations to my family, the comfort of a consistent paycheck, and the impending monthly financial commitments, the idea of letting go was unsettling. Inborn talent, unrelenting enthusiasm, and an undeniable hunger to live out my true purpose, however, lured me onward. It was challenging at first. I had to rely on my savings and an unemployment paycheck to get me through the first several months, but I was determined, focused and persistent.

When you have a clear and specific goal in mind, your thoughts naturally align with that goal. Visualizing your desired outcome and maintaining a focused mindset can help you stay motivated and on track. For the past decade, I've established a morning ritual. I wake up at 5 am, enjoy a cup of coffee, spend 15 minutes reading business books, and then dive into an intense outdoor workout. This routine has remained constant despite the difficulties that come with navigating through uncertain times. I can say with confidence that this practice has been crucial in helping me maintain my discipline and attention, acting as a cornerstone in my mission to realize my aspirations.

SECRET # 10

Self-doubt and insecurity can often stall progress, trapping us in a cycle. Building self-assurance through positive self-talk and affirmations can help you overcome self-imposed limitations and take bold actions toward your goals.

Sometimes, you might need to shift from a fixed mindset ("I can't do this") to a growth mindset ("I can learn and improve"). Embracing challenges and setbacks as opportunities for growth can help you persevere.

Believing that you can achieve whatever career goal you have set is the first step. It is, however, no substitute for action. While positive thoughts are essential, they must be coupled with intentional actions and a well-defined plan. Regularly evaluate your progress, adjust your strategies as needed, and continue nurturing a positive mindset to help you overcome obstacles and achieve your goals.

In closing, keep in mind that your search for the ideal career involves more than just looking for a job; it also involves pursuing your passions and objectives. You now possess the knowledge, tactics, and frame of mind necessary to successfully negotiate the job-hunting environment thanks to this book.

As you step forward into the world of opportunities, embrace the challenges with enthusiasm and perseverance. Every failure is a learning experience for resiliency, and every success is evidence of your commitment. Remember that success is not necessarily a straight line but rather the accumulation of knowledge gained, and abilities developed. Maintain a proactive approach to networking, skill development, and job market adaptation. Believe in your special talents and the value you contribute. The appropriate opportunity is out there waiting for you, so have faith in the process and practice patience. Remember, you are not defined by the number of applications you send out, but by the determination you exhibit and the growth you experience throughout this journey. Your dream job is not just a destination but a milestone in your lifelong pursuit of growth and fulfillment.

So, go forth with confidence, fueled by the knowledge within these pages and the fire within your heart. The path ahead might have twists and turns, but each step you take brings you closer to the realization of your goals. Your future is bright, and your potential is limitless.

Best of luck in your job-hunting adventure!

Chapter 11

KEY TAKEAWAYS

1. **Lay a Firm Foundation:**

    a. Craft a well-structured resume that highlights your skills, accomplishments, and relevant experiences.
    b. Draft an engaging single-page cover letter that does not replicate your resume.
    c. Create a compelling online presence through LinkedIn and other professional platforms.

2. **BrandYou and Network:**

    a. Showcase your expertise and personality through consistent online and offline personal branding.
    b. Develop a strong professional network by attending events, joining industry groups, and leveraging social media.

3. **Search Strategically:**

 a. Understand your strengths, interests, and career goals and target suitable job opportunities.
 b. Utilize a combination of online job boards, networking, and direct applications for a well-rounded job search approach.

4. **Prepare for the Interview:**

 a. Research the company and role thoroughly to demonstrate your genuine interest and knowledge.
 b. Practice answering common interview questions and prepare thoughtful questions to ask the interviewer.

5. **Nail the Interview:**

 a. Showcase your skills and experiences by providing specific examples and results.
 b. Demonstrate your enthusiasm, adaptability, and cultural fit with the company.

6. **Follow Up:**

 a. Send a personalized thank-you email after the interview to express appreciation and restate your interest.
 b. Keep communication channels open while respecting the company's timeline for decision-making.

7. **Negotiate Job Offers:**

a. Research industry standards and salary ranges to negotiate a fair compensation package.
b. Consider factors beyond salary, such as benefits, work-life balance, and career growth opportunities.

8. **Manage Rejections and Setbacks:**

a. Don't be discouraged by rejections; treat them as learning opportunities.
b. Seek feedback, make necessary improvements, and persist in your job search efforts.

9. **Continue Learning:**

a. Invest in ongoing skill development and education to stay competitive in your field.
b. Keep refining your job-hunting strategies based on changing global market conditions.

10. **Believe You Can and You Are Half-Way There**

a. Your thoughts are in your total control. They can either propel you toward success or hold you back.
b. Embrace the challenges with enthusiasm and perseverance.

LET'S CONNECT!

As an author, I'm truly grateful for your support and enthusiasm for my work. Writing is a journey that becomes even more meaningful when shared with readers like you.

I'd love to connect with you on social media and create a space where we can engage, share thoughts, and build a community around our shared love for employability skills, business, entrepreneurship, and personal development. Let's embark on this adventure together! Here's how we can stay connected:

▌ **Follow Me:** Make sure to follow me on my favorite business platform, LinkedIn @AndriePenta. I'll be sharing sneak peeks of upcoming projects, behind-the-scenes glimpses into my training work, and maybe even some personal tidbits from time to time.

💬 **Engage and Connect:** Don't be shy! Comment on my posts, send me messages, and share your own business endeavors. This is a space for genuine connections and engaging conversations. Should you wish to connect via email, please do so on: andriepenta@gmail.com or apenta@doortraining.cy.

ACKNOWLEDGMENTS

I would like to extend my heartfelt acknowledgments to my family for their support throughout the writing of this book. Your encouragement, understanding, and belief in me have been the pillars that held me up during the writing process.

To my husband: your willingness to lend a helping hand has been a true blessing.

This is not just my accomplishment; it is a testament to the collective support and love that surrounds me. Thank you for being my pillars of strength and for standing by me as I pursued this creative endeavor. Your support has made this journey richer.

With heartfelt gratitude,

Andrie

LEAVE A REVIEW

If you've enjoyed this book and found it valuable, I would greatly appreciate it if you could take a moment to leave a review on Amazon. Your feedback helps me improve and assists other readers in discovering the benefits within these pages.

Thank you for being a part of my literary journey.

ABOUT THE AUTHOR

Andrie studied Marketing and Business Management in London where she also acquired the Advanced Certificate from the Chartered Institute of Marketing London. She oversaw marketing and communications at EY Cyprus until 2008. At the same time, she graduated with Distinction from London and was awarded a Master's degree in Strategic Marketing. In 2008, she founded Penta Marketing Art, which provided marketing and public relations solutions for private and public companies. In 2010, she founded the Cyprus Image Institute after obtaining the title of Certified Image Maker (with attendance in London) and joined as an associate member of the Association of Image Consultants International. At 27, Andrie was the youngest nominated Ambassador for Female Entrepreneurship for Europe, serving since then as a business advisor and mentor. In 2013, Andrie was designated as the Goodwill Ambassador of the Hope in Life Foundation and a Cypriot Woman of the Year (2013) finalist. She enjoys regular and extensive publicity in local print, online and television programs, and have been interviewed for various publications in Cyprus, US, Denmark, Holland and Greece. She was a Senior Manager at the Markets department of KPMG in Cyprus, and she held the role of the Leader of the Ronald McDonald House Charities of Cyprus until 2022. She has since then ascended to the esteemed rank of Master Trainer and Consultant, proudly affiliated with the renowned global training powerhouse, Door Training and Consulting. Andrie is a Certified trainer by the Human Resource Development Authority of Cyprus. Her areas of expertise include Employability Skills, Building Teams, Management, Leadership, Negotiations, Communication, Customer Experience, Sales, Public Speaking and Media Training. She delivers training in Greek and English.

www.ingramcontent.com/pod-product-compliance
Lightning Source LLC
Chambersburg PA
CBHW062250290526
45794CB00006B/2494